MW00973466

This Journal belongs to

_____

DATE:

From _____ to _____

First printing: August 2016

Copyright © 2016 by Answers in Genesis–USA. All rights reserved. No part of this book may be used or reproduced in any manner whatsoever without written permission of the publisher, except in the case of brief quotations in articles and reviews. For information write:

Master Books®, P.O. Box 726, Green Forest, AR 72638

Master Books® is a division of the New Leaf Publishing Group, Inc.

ISBN: 978-0-89051-936-3

Unless otherwise noted, Scripture quotations are from the King James Version of the Bible.

Scripture taken from the New King James Version®. Copyright © 1982 by Thomas Nelson. Used by permission. All rights reserved.

Printed in the United States of America

Please visit our website for other great titles:
www.masterbooks.com

For information regarding interviews,
please contact the publicity department at (870) 438-5288

Master Books®
A Division of New Leaf Publishing Group
www.masterbooks.com

EXPEDITION ARK
Noah's Journey of Faith

PreFlood Map

Now all the writers of barbarian histories make mention of this flood, and of this ark; among whom is Berosus the Chaldean. For when he is describing the circumstances of the flood, he goes on thus: "It is said there is still some part of this ship in Armenia, at the mountain of the Cordyaeans; and that some people carry off pieces of the bitumen, which they take away, and use chiefly as amulets for the averting of mischiefs." Hieronymus the Egyptian also, who wrote the Phoenician Antiquities, and Mnaseas, and a great many more, make mention of the same.

−ANTIQUITIES OF THE JEWS BOOK 1, CHAPTER 3. BY FLAVIUS JOSEPHUS

... NOAH WAS A JUST MAN AND PERFECT IN HIS GENERATIONS, AND NOAH WALKED WITH GOD. ——GENESIS 6:9

> Noah was very uneasy at what they did; and being displeased at their conduct, persuaded them to change their dispositions and their acts for the better: but seeing they did not yield to him, but were slaves to their wicked pleasures, he was afraid they would kill him, together with his wife and children, and those they had married; so he departed out of that land.
> —*ANTIQUITIES OF THE JEWS* BOOK 1, CHAPTER 3

The words spoken by Lamech, Noah's father, may indicate that he worked hard at farming the land. Thus, Noah may have learned how to plant crops and care for animals at an early age. The name Noah means "rest" and his father hoped that he would bring rest from their hard work because of the curse on the ground. Noah was born a little more than a thousand years after God created everything, and the enormous task of building the Ark and caring for the animals likely required a variety of skills, such as growing crops, animal husbandry, woodworking, metalworking, and leadership.

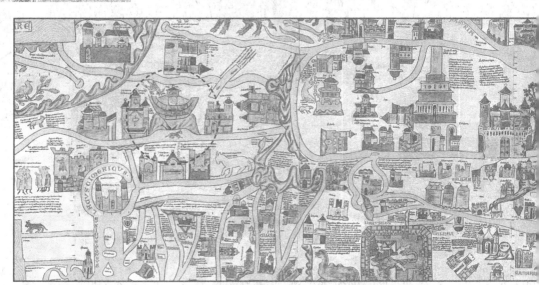

EBSTORFER WORLD MAP: ORIGINALLY DATED TO THE 13TH CENTURY AND MEASURING ALMOST 12 FEET SQUARE, THE EBSTORFER MAP WAS DISCOVERED IN 1843 AND DESTROYED DURING WORLD WAR II. THE IMAGE OF THE ARK ON THE MOUNTAINS INCLUDES THE DOVE RETURNING.

For this is as the waters of Noah unto me: for as I
have sworn that the waters of Noah should no more
go over the earth; so have I sworn that I would not
be wroth with thee, nor rebuke thee.

——Isaiah 54:9

BUT AS THE DAYS OF NOAH WERE, SO SHALL ALSO THE
COMING OF THE SON OF MAN BE.

——MATTHEW 24:37

THERE WENT IN TWO AND TWO UNTO NOAH INTO THE ARK,
THE MALE AND THE FEMALE, AS GOD HAD COMMANDED NOAH.
——GENESIS 7:9

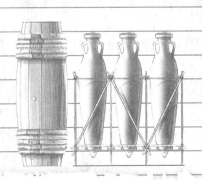

And God said unto Noah, The end of all flesh is come
before me; for the earth is filled with violence
through them; and, behold, I will destroy them with
the earth.   ——Genesis 6:13

And, behold, I, even I, do bring a flood of waters upon the earth, to destroy all flesh, wherein is the breath of life, from under heaven; and every thing that is in the earth shall die. ——Genesis 6:17

But with thee will I establish my covenant; and thou shalt come into the ark, thou, and thy sons, and thy wife, and thy sons' wives with thee.

——Genesis 6:18

> When God gave the signal, and it began to rain,
> the water poured down forty entire days, till
> it became fifteen cubits higher than the earth;
> which was the reason why there was no greater
> number preserved, since they had no place to
> fly to. When the rain ceased, the water did but
> just begin to abate after one hundred and fifty
> days, (that is, on the seventeenth day of the
> seventh month,) it then ceasing to subside for a
> little while. After this, the ark rested on the top
> of a certain mountain in Armenia.
> —*ANTIQUITIES OF THE JEWS* BOOK 1, CHAPTER 3

How could Noah have learned the skills he needed to
build the Ark? We know that God gives each person
the talents and abilities to accomplish the purpose He
assigns them. Like people today, Noah surely developed
his God-given abilities throughout his lifetime. He
clearly learned how to work with wood, and he may
have also been trained to work with metals to make
tools and braces for the construction of the Ark.
Perhaps driven by a desire for adventure and a love for
construction, Noah may have traveled to a small port
city, becoming an apprentice shipwright. Here he could
have learned blacksmithing and shipbuilding.

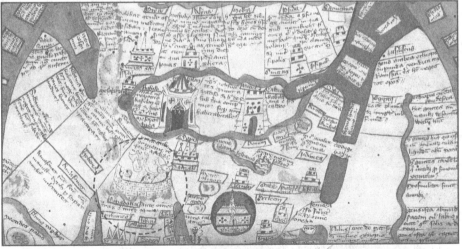

RANULF HIGDEN WORLD MAP : THIS MAP FROM THE 14TH CENTURY HAS JERUSALEM AT THE CENTER, A COMMON
PRACTICE AMONG SOME MAPMAKERS OF THAT TIME. NOAH IS DEPICTED IN HIS ARK WITH THREE DIFFERENT ANIMALS.

And of every living thing of all flesh, two of every sort shalt thou bring into the ark, to keep them alive with thee; they shall be male and female.

——Genesis 6:19

Thus did Noah; according to all that God commanded him, so did he.

——Genesis 6:22

And the LORD said unto Noah, Come thou and all thy house into the ark; for thee have I seen righteous before me in this generation.

——Genesis 7:1

And Noah did according unto all that the LORD
commanded him.

—Genesis 7:5

And Noah was six hundred years old when the flood of waters was upon the earth.

——Genesis 7:6

And Noah went in, and his sons, and his wife, and his sons' wives with him, into the ark, because of the waters of the flood.

—Genesis 7:7

And Noah begat three sons, Shem, Ham, and Japheth. ——Genesis 6:10

Noah learned that the earth was become clear of the flood. So after he had staid seven more days, he sent the living creatures out of the ark; and both he and his family went out, when he also sacrificed to God, and feasted with his companions. However, the Armenians call this place, The Place of Descent; for the ark being saved in that place, its remains are shown there by the inhabitants to this day.
–*ANTIQUITIES OF THE JEWS* BOOK 1, CHAPTER 3

Noah lived in an increasingly evil world, yet he faithfully served the Lord. Rejecting the wickedness in his city, Noah boldly proclaimed the truth about God. He was a just man, and he walked with God. At 500 years of age, Noah and his wife had the first of their sons. Before long, Shem, Ham, and Japheth had each married a wife. With so few godly people left on the planet, Noah's righteous ways may have brought derision and hatred from his neighbors.

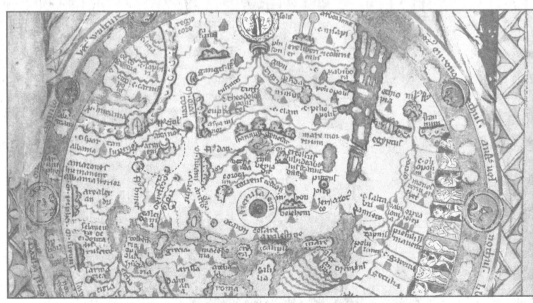

PSALTER WORLD MAP: THIS MEDIEVAL MAP IS BELIEVED TO HAVE BEEN MADE IN THE 13TH CENTURY. JESUS IS SHOWN AT THE TOP, JERUSALEM AT THE CENTER, AND THE SIMPLE DRAWING OF THE ARK ON THE MOUNTAINTOP.

In the six hundredth year of Noah's life, in the second month, the seventeenth day of the month, the same day were all the fountains of the great deep broken up, and the windows of heaven were opened.

—Genesis 7:11

And they went in unto Noah into the ark, two and
two of all flesh, wherein is the breath of life.

——Genesis 7:15

DATE   /   /   LOCATION

And the flood was forty days upon the earth; and the waters increased, and bare up the ark, and it was lift up above the earth.

——Genesis 7:17

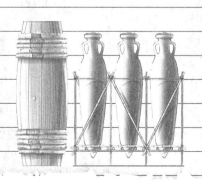

And the waters prevailed exceedingly upon the earth; and all the high hills, that were under the whole heaven, were covered.

—Genesis 7:19

And the waters prevailed upon the earth an hundred and fifty days.

——Genesis 7:24

And God remembered Noah, and every living thing, and
all the cattle that was with him in the ark: and God
made a wind to pass over the earth, and the waters
assuaged.

——Genesis 8:1

And he called his name Noah, saying, This same shall comfort us concerning our work and toil of our hands, because of the ground which the LORD hath cursed. ——Genesis 5:29

Nicolaus of Damascus, in his ninety-sixth book, hath a particular relation about them; where he speaks thus: "There is a great mountain in Armenia, over Minyas, called Baris, upon which it is reported that many who fled at the time of the Deluge were saved; and that one who was carried in an ark came on shore upon the top of it; and that the remains of the timber were a great while preserved. This might be the man about whom Moses the legislator of the Jews wrote."
—*ANTIQUITIES OF THE JEWS* BOOK 1, CHAPTER 3

The Ark was made of gopherwood, a species unidentified in our time. Noah was instructed to cover it with pitch, both inside and out. The word translated as Ark is a loan word that is also used for the small basket in which the infant Moses was placed to float on the river. Contrary to certain claims, the word does not express the shape of the object. Rather, it seems to describe its function: an ark is something used to preserve life

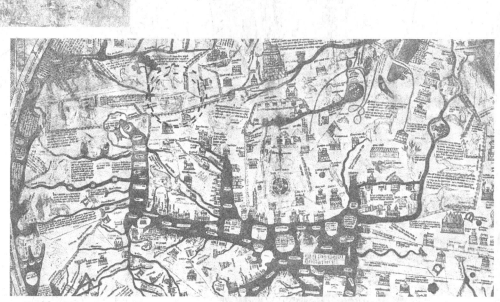

Hereford Mappa Mundi : Believed to be from the 13th century, this is considered the largest surviving medieval map, which includes Jerusalem at the center, with the Garden of Eden and Noah's Ark.

AND THE ARK RESTED IN THE SEVENTH MONTH, ON THE
SEVENTEENTH DAY OF THE MONTH, UPON THE MOUNTAINS OF
ARARAT.

——GENESIS 8:4

And the waters decreased continually until the tenth month: in the tenth month, on the first day of the month, were the tops of the mountains seen.

——Genesis 8:5

And the dove came in to him in the evening; and, lo, in her mouth was an olive leaf pluckt off: so Noah knew that the waters were abated from off the earth.

——Genesis 8:11

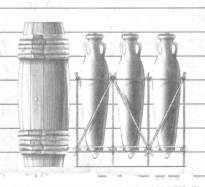

AND IT CAME TO PASS IN THE SIX HUNDREDTH AND FIRST YEAR, IN THE FIRST MONTH, THE FIRST DAY OF THE MONTH, THE WATERS WERE DRIED UP FROM OFF THE EARTH: AND NOAH REMOVED THE COVERING OF THE ARK, AND LOOKED, AND, BEHOLD, THE FACE OF THE GROUND WAS DRY.   —GENESIS 8:13

And God spake unto Noah, saying, Go forth of the ark, thou, and thy wife, and thy sons, and thy sons' wives with thee.

——Genesis 8:15–16

And Noah went forth, and his sons, and his wife, and his sons' wives with him.

——Genesis 8:18

MAKE THEE AN ARK OF GOPHER WOOD; ROOMS SHALT THOU MAKE IN THE ARK, AND SHALT PITCH IT WITHIN AND WITHOUT WITH PITCH. ——GENESIS 6:14

He also entreated God to accept of his sacrifice, and to grant that the earth might never again undergo the like effects of his wrath; that men might be permitted to go on cheerfully in cultivating the same; to build cities, and live happily in them; and that they might not be deprived of any of those good things which they enjoyed before the Flood; but might attain to the like length of days, and old age, which the ancient people had arrived at before.

–ANTIQUITIES OF THE JEWS BOOK 1, CHAPTER 3

Noah faithfully accomplished the undertaking God set before him. The years of shedding blood, sweat, and tears while working on the Ark had finally come to an end. After loading all the land animals and cargo onto the Ark, Noah and his family paused to thank the Lord for His provision and took in their final glimpse of sunlight before the Flood. From early history, men like Tubal-Cain worked with bronze and iron, but the Flood buried the sources of metallic ores. As Noah's descendants began to populate the earth, metals needed to be rediscovered and technologies lost had to be reinvented.

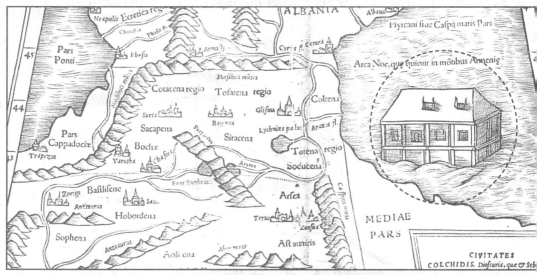

TABULA ASIAE III : ON THIS ANCIENT MAP ONE CAN SEE NOAH'S ARK PROMINENTLY FLOATING IN THE CASPIAN SEA MOVING TOWARD ITS EVENTUAL LANDING SPOT THOUGHT TO HAVE BEEN IN ARMENIA DURING THE GREAT FLOOD.

EVERY BEAST, EVERY CREEPING THING, AND EVERY FOWL, AND WHATSOEVER CREEPETH UPON THE EARTH, AFTER THEIR KINDS, WENT FORTH OUT OF THE ARK.

——GENESIS 8:19

DATE / / LOCATION

And Noah builded an altar unto the LORD; and took
of every clean beast, and of every clean fowl, and
offered burnt offerings on the altar.
——Genesis 8:20

And the LORD smelled a sweet savour; and the LORD said in his heart, I will not again curse the ground any more for man's sake; for the imagination of man's heart is evil from his youth; neither will I again smite any more every thing living, as I have done. ——GENESIS 8:21

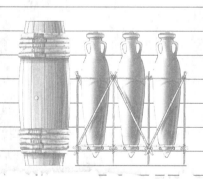

WHILE THE EARTH REMAINETH, SEEDTIME AND HARVEST, AND COLD AND HEAT, AND SUMMER AND WINTER, AND DAY AND NIGHT SHALL NOT CEASE.

——GENESIS 8:22

And God blessed Noah and his sons, and said unto them, Be fruitful, and multiply, and replenish the earth.
—Genesis 9:1

And I, behold, I establish my covenant with you, and
with your seed after you.

———Genesis 9:9

For as in the days that were before the flood they were eating and drinking, marrying and giving in marriage, until the day that Noah entered into the ark. —— Matthew 24:38

When Noah had made these supplications,
God, who loved the man for his righteousness,
granted entire success to his prayers, and said,
that it was not he who brought the destruction on a polluted world, but that they under-
went that vengeance on account of their own
wickedness; and that he had not brought men
into the world if he had himself determined
to destroy them, it being an instance of great-
er wisdom not to have granted them life at
all, than, after it was granted, to procure their
destruction.
　　　　　—*ANTIQUITIES OF THE JEWS* BOOK 1, CHAPTER 3

People despised their own Creator. Lust for
power and a desire for sensuality in all forms
flourished. The world was thoroughly infested
with violence, idolatry, and every imaginable
form of immorality. On the tenth day of the
second month in Noah's 600th year, God
commanded him to enter the Ark with his
family and the animals. Seven days later, as
Noah finished loading the Ark, the Flood began
and caught an unsuspecting world by surprise.

GEORGIE ARMENIE MAP: THIS 17TH-CENTURY MAP
OF ARMENIA AND GEORGE INCLUDES MT. ARARAT
AND A TINY ARK IMAGE. IN MANY EARLY MAPS,
ARMENIA INCLUDED NOAH'S ARK.

And I will establish my covenant with you, neither shall all flesh be cut off any more by the waters of a flood; neither shall there any more be a flood to destroy the earth. ——Genesis 9:11

And God said, This is the token of the covenant which I
make between me and you and every living creature that
is with you, for perpetual generations: I do set my bow
in the cloud, and it shall be for a token of a covenant
between me and the earth.   —Genesis 9:12-13

THEY DID EAT, THEY DRANK, THEY MARRIED WIVES, THEY
WERE GIVEN IN MARRIAGE, UNTIL THE DAY THAT NOAH
ENTERED INTO THE ARK, AND THE FLOOD CAME, AND
DESTROYED THEM ALL.   —LUKE 17:27

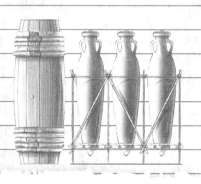

By faith Noah, being warned of God of things not seen
as yet, moved with fear, prepared an ark to the saving
of his house; by the which he condemned the world,
and became heir of the righteousness which is by faith.
——Hebrews 11:7

DATE / /   LOCATION

WHICH SOMETIME WERE DISOBEDIENT, WHEN ONCE THE
LONGSUFFERING OF GOD WAITED IN THE DAYS OF NOAH, WHILE
THE ARK WAS A PREPARING, WHEREIN FEW, THAT IS, EIGHT
SOULS WERE SAVED BY WATER.   ——1 PETER 3:20

AND DID NOT SPARE THE ANCIENT WORLD, BUT SAVED NOAH,
ONE OF EIGHT PEOPLE, A PREACHER OF RIGHTEOUSNESS,
BRINGING IN THE FLOOD ON THE WORLD OF THE UNGODLY.
——2 PETER 2:5 (NKJV)

NEW **ARK** RESOURC
ENCOUNTER®

HOW MANY ANIMALS WERE ON THE ARK?
978-0-89051-935-6
$15.99 U.S.

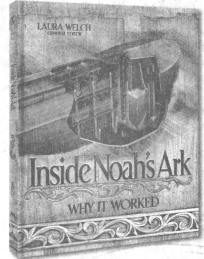

INSIDE NOA
978-0-89051
$16.99 U.S.

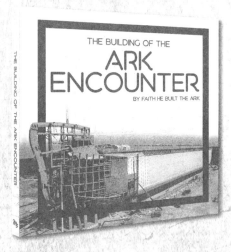

THE BUILDING OF THE ARK ENCOUNTER
978-0-89051-931-8
$17.99 U.S.

To order or request a catalog:

New Leaf Publishing Group
PO Box 726, Green Forest, AR 72638